1

Lending

A

Helping

Hand

Vol. 48

Charles Preston Fletcher

Help Someone,

Not for the reward,

But for the sake

Of

CHANGING A LIFE.

Helping Other People

Can Be a Cure,

Not Just for Those

Who Are In Need,

But for Your Soul

As Well.

Fill Your Mind
With Truth
Fill Your Heart
With Love
Fill Your Life
With Service.

Remember
If You Ever Need
A Helping Hand, It is at
the End of Your Arm.
As You Get Older,
Remember You Have
Another Hand. The
First is to Help Yourself,
the Second
Is to Help Others.

The best helping hand

That you will ever

receive is the one

At the end of your

Own arm.

We Can't Help Everyone, But Everyone Can Help Someone

To serve is beautiful,

But only

If it is done

With Joy

And a Whole

Heart

When Ever

You Can

Lend a Helping Hand

Take the time

To understand

And lend a

Gentle helping

Hand.

Our

Prime

Purpose

In Life

Is To

Help Others.

Give

Your Hands

To Serve

And

Your Hearts

To Love.

Helping

The weak

Will

Make You

STRONG

My hands

Can only reach

So far.

Take my hand,

And together

We can reach

So much

Further.

There is no

Better way

To thank God

For your sight

Than by giving

A helping hand

To someone

In the dark.

There is

No better

Exercise for the heart

Than

Reaching down

And picking

People up.

The first

To help you up

Are the ones

Who know

How it feels

To fall down.

HELPING

HANDS

ARE

BETTER THAN

PRAYING

LIPS

Even if it's a little

Thing, do something

For those who have

Need of a man's help,

Something for which

You get no pay

But the privilege

Of doing it.

For remember,

You don't live in a world

Of your own.

Your brothers

Are here too.

NEVER LOOK

DOWN

ON ANYBODY

UNLESS

YOU ARE

HELPING

HIM UP.

No One

Has Ever

Become Poor

By Giving.

Helping show another
Their potential helps
them see that all
things are possible.

Many Hands

Make

Light Work

You must be

The change

You wish to see

In the world.

Get to know

Your neighbor

And be there

For them

With your arm

Extended

Ready to lend

A helping hand.

Help others

Achieve Their

Dreams and

You will

Achieve yours.

Help a person

In need

And you will both

Succeed

Kindness is one of the

Greatest gifts you can

Bestow upon another.

If someone is in need,

Lend them a helping hand.

Do not wait for a thank you.

True kindness lies within

The act of giving without

The expectation of

Something in return.

Earn your success

Based on service

To others, not

At the expense

Of others.

Helping others

and

Encouraging others,

Are often acts of

Being kind that have

More meaning

Than you may

Realize.

HELP someone,
Not for the reward,
But for the sake of
CHANGING A LIFE.

A kind gesture

Can reach a wound

That only

Compassion

Can heal.

Every single
Time you help
Somebody
Stand up, you
Are helping
Humanity
Rise.

Helping Hands

Fit those of Others

No matter what

Their Age, Size, or Color.

Extend a
Helping hand
To people
Around you.

We make a living

By what we get,

But we make

A life by

What we give.

My hands

Can only reach

So far.

Take my hand,

And together

We can reach

So much further.

Be a hand

That reaches out.

Be a smile for those

Who have no reason

To smile.

Be a light for those

Who live in darkness.

Show them what

It means to truly love.

A FRIEND is he

Who gives a

Helping hand

To his FRIEND

In distress.

Make it your

Business to reach out

To others and help.

IF YOU MEET
SOMEONE
WHO HAS NO SMILE,
GIVE THEM
ONE OF YOURS.

A friend will offer

A helping hand

Whenever you

Are down

And guide you

Through the darkness

Till the light

Your heart has found.

Gratitude

Makes sense

Of our past,

Brings peace

For today, and

Creates a vision

For tomorrow.

God lends

A helping hand

To the one

Who tries

Hard.

HELPING

Is helping

Even when

It feels

Like a drop

In the ocean.

One of the best

Feelings in the

World is knowing

That someone

Is happy

Because of you.

When we

Follow our bliss,

We are met

By a thousand

Unseen

Helping hands.

A person's most

Useful asset

Is not the

Head full of

knowledge, but a

Heart full of love,

An ear ready to

Listen and a hand

Willing to help.

Lend a helping hand

Encourage

Always Listen

Do the right thing

Energize

Respect others

Serve

Helping Hands

Spread Love

Around the World

In times of tragedies,

Our duty is to lend

A helping hand to those

In grief and thus

Light lamps

Of Kindness

And

Compassion.

YOU GIVE BUT
LITTLE WHEN YOU
GIVE OF YOUR
POSSESSIONS. IT IS
WHEN YOU GIVE
OF YOURSELF
THAT YOU
TRULY GIVE.

GIVING

IS ONE

OF LIFE'S

GREATEST

JOYS

Heal the world!

Stop the hate.

Lend a Helping Hand

To those in need.

Lend a
Helping Hand.

Together
We Can.

EVERYONE IS
FIGHTING THEIR
OWN BATTLE,
NO MATTER
HOW BIG OR SMALL
...LET'S HELP
EACH OTHER
ALONG.

WE CAN'T HELP EVERYONE, BUT EVERYONE CAN HELP SOMEONE.

What is the

Essence of life?

To serve others

And do good.

Loving

Means

Lending

A Hand

Whether it be the giving of the Helping Hand itself,

Or the giving of the gratitude for the help

That the Helping Hand provides.

Be a lamp,

A lifeboat,

A ladder.

Help

Someone's

Soul heal.

Whenever you need

Any help, remember

I am ready

To lend a hand.

Call me.

A person's most

Useful asset is not a

Head full of knowledge,

But a heart full of love,

An ear ready to listen

And a hand

Willing to help others.

Lending a hand,

In big or small ways,

Is giving hope and care

In big ways.

Have a Heart.

Lend a hand.

Make a
Difference.

Changing

The World

Always

Needs

Volunteers.

A Good Deed

BRIGHTENS

A dark

WORLD

Life's
Persistent
And
Most urgent
Question is,
What are You
Doing for Others?

All Things are

Possible

To Him Who

Believes!

HEAL THE
WORLD!
STOP THE HATE.
LEND A
HELPING HAND
TO THOSE
IN NEED.

Today...Smile
Express a word of
Kindness, lend a
Helping hand, write
A note of gratitude,
Give a word
Of encouragement.

We work on
ourselves
In order to
help others, but also
we help others
in order to
work on ourselves.

My hands

Can only reach

So far, take my hand

And together

We can reach

So much further.

The possibilities

For us

To lend a hand

And be a friend

Are endless.

A Helping Hand

Can Vastly Increase

The Range of Possibilities

That is Possible

When two People

Work Together

As "ONE".

I want to help inspire you to be a better person by Helping Others and Getting Nothing in Return.

A Helping Hand!
HOW FAR SHOULD
WE GO?

That's Easy:

"As Far

As Our Arms

Can Reach &

As Long as

Our Hearts

Feel the Need

To Help"

Doing something for someone else simply out of the kindness of your heart speaks volumes about who you are as a person. When we help others, it gives them a chance to shine, and you never know just how much that could mean to them when they are feeling low. This collection of quotes about helping others will inspire you to lend a helping hand for nothing in return.

Helping others without expecting anything in return can bring lasting happiness. It can help you build long-lasting relationships, open more doors for you, and bring meaningful success.

Living for others helps you find great freedom and inner peace. Remember, true joy and fulfillment is found not in being served, but in choosing to serve.

Although most people today are motivated by what they get in return, we should learn to help with no expectation of repayment; for we shall be repaid with joy and fulfillment in countless other ways.

The purpose of life is not to be happy. It is to be useful, to be honorable, to be compassionate, to have it make some difference that you have lived and lived well.

There is no exercise better for the heart than reaching down and lifting people up.

You have not lived today until you have done something for someone who can never repay you.

A kind gesture can reach a wound that only compassion can heal.

I don't want to live in the kind of world where we don't look out for each other. Not just the people that are close to us, but anybody who needs a helping hand. I can't change the way anybody else thinks, or what they choose to do, but I can do my bit.

There is nothing more beautiful than someone who goes out of their way to make life beautiful for others.

It's not enough to have lived. We should be determined to live for something. May I suggest that it be creating joy for others, sharing what we have for the betterment of person kind, bringing hope to the lost and love to the lonely.

If you're not making someone else's life better, then you're wasting your time. Your life will become better by making other lives better.

I'm starting to think this world is just a place for us to learn that we need each other more than we want to admit.

Those who are happiest are those who do the most for others.

One of the most important things you can do on this earth is to let people know they are not alone.

Never underestimate the difference YOU can make in the lives of others. Step forward, reach out and help. This week reach to someone that might need a lift.

The next time you want to withhold your help, or your love, or your support for another for whatever the reason, ask yourself a simple question: do the reasons you want to withhold it reflect more on them or on you? And which reasons do you want defining you forevermore?

Remember this. Hold on to this. This is the only perfection there is, the perfection of helping others. This is the only thing we can do that has any lasting meaning. This is why we're here. To make each other feel safe.

Service to humanity is service to God.

Stand up for someone who is in need so that it will build confidence in you to stand up for yourself at times when required…

The simple gift of giving becomes an elaborate rich aftertaste of a natural blissful feeling, lingering endlessly in my lifetime.

When you reach out to those in need, do not be surprised if the essential meaning of something occurs.

Sometimes, we may discover we helped the wrong person, but that should not be a reason to stop helping other people in need, even though we were fooled previously. If you want to do good, there are opportunities everywhere. Don't let the fools spoil your good heart.

It is literally true that you can succeed best and quickest by helping others to succeed.

Let the echo of your footsteps spark a ray of hope in the heart of the hopeless and appear as help to the helpless.

Never suppress a generous thought.

Every shine which destroys the darkness of others is a holy shine!

When the chance comes to do a good deed, don't waste it because it might never come back. The world doesn't have an (Undo) button; still, you have your conscience, brain, wisdom, and heart to help you do the right thing.

When you help someone, you also help yourself. Instead of worrying about how much you get in return, you are better off helping as many people as you can.

Helping others is a good effort to instill human dignity.

Our prime purpose in life is to help others. If you can't help them, at least do not hurt them.

Ask not what I can get more from others, but instead what gift I have that can better help serve others more.

Being able to uplift others is the biggest miracle in the world.

The most fulfilling times in my life are those times when I am helping others.

Be nice to people… maybe it'll be unappreciated, unreciprocated, or ignored, but spread the love anyway. We rise by lifting others.

Focus on building up others, and your own sense of self-worth will improve. Some call these random acts of human kindness. But the truth is, acting unselfishly is not random at all. Instead, it is a conscious, concerted effort to make the world better by making someone else's life better. The bonus: you will be happier by doing it.

You can raise your potential when you help someone to reach their potential.

Success comes in direct proportion to the number of people you help.

Don't value your self-worth by others or external things but by appreciating who you are within. And if you must measure your success do it not by what you have gained personally but what you have contributed to a wider benefit.

A truly successful person is not one who achieves his highest ambitions, but one who enjoys helping others reach theirs.

If you are truly concerned about helping people and creating value for them in your business and life. God will take care of you, and the universe will reward you.

Find out how much God has given you and from it take what you need; the remainder is needed by others.

Help others and give something back. I guarantee you will discover that while public service improves the lives and the world around you, its greatest reward is the enrichment and new meaning it will bring your own life.

Thousands of candles can be lighted from a single candle, and the life of the candle will not be shortened. Happiness never decreases by being shared.

What we have done for ourselves alone dies with us; what we have done for others and the world remains and is immortal.

The work an unknown good man has done is like a vein of water flowing hidden underground, secretly making the ground green.

Let no one ever come to you without leaving better and happier. Be the living expression of God's kindness: kindness in your face, kindness in your eyes, kindness in your smile.

When you dig another out of their troubles, you find a place to bury your own.

Our greatness has always come from people who expect nothing and take nothing for granted – folks who work hard for what they have, then reach back and help others after them.

To me, there are saints every day. They stand up and help others and live for others and do things for others.

The main rule to me is to honor God with your life. To live a life of integrity. Not be selfish. You know, help others. But that's really the essence of the Christian faith.

No one is useless in this world who lightens the burdens of another.

You need an attitude of service. You're not just serving yourself. You help others to grow up and you grow with them.

An effort made for the happiness of others lifts us above ourselves.

People who need our help exist all around us. When you help them, it means you've done something to help them move forward.

Helping other people reach their goals can result in you achieving your own success as well.

Stop Bullying Now!

Take a Stand

Lend a Hand

Together

We Have

The Power.

Everyone

Is fighting

Their own battle,

No matter

How big or small...

Let's Help Each

Other along.

Lending a Hand...

It is being there

For people because

You know what

It is like

To have no one

There for you.

Be a hand

that reaches out.

Be a smile for those

Who have no reason

To smile.

Be a light for those

Who live in darkness.

Show them what

It means to truly

Love.

We who are strong

Ought to bear the

Weaknesses

Of the weak.

Lend a Helping Hand

To someone

With Autism.

Real generosity

Is doing

Something nice

For someone

Who will

Never find out.

Be a Friend

Lend a Hand

Reach Out

Say "Stop"

Report Concerns

Never worry about

Numbers. Help One

Person at a time

And always start

With the person

Nearest you.

They're not looking for a handout. They're not looking for a freebee. They're really looking for a helping hand. They have ambition. They're bright people. And by the stroke of chance, they ended up with a need.

Life is too short

Not to create,

Not to love,

And not to

Lend a helping hand

To Our

Brothers and sisters.

Give your hands

To SERVE

And your hearts

To LOVE.

A kind gesture

Can reach a wound

That only

Compassion

Can heal.

It was on my fifth birthday that Papa put his hand on my shoulder and said, Remember, my son, if you ever need a helping hand, you'll find one at the end of your arm.

Our actions

Towards others

Should not be

About pointing

Fingers but, about

Offering a

Helping hand, instead

Lend a helping hand

To one who needs

Assistance but,

Doesn't know

Where to get it.

If a natural disaster
Strikes your community,
Reach out
To your friends,
Neighbors, and
Complete strangers.
With a much needed, and
highly appreciated, helping
Hand you can make
A world of difference.

The impersonal

Hand of government

Can never replace

The helping hand

Of a neighbor.

There are people

Who help you in life.

I've been given a helping

Hand, and that's why I

Feel it's my duty to help

Others as well.

If you can stretch

Out a helping hand...

Don't hesitate

Just do it.

Sometimes we need
To go beyond just
offering a helping hand

Like when we need to
shed tears and share
hugs with those who

In a matter of just a few
hours, lost everything to
the rising

Floodwaters.

No man is self-made.

The amount of help,

And people, that you
sometimes need to lend
you a helping hand to
get ahead in the world

Is sometimes

Extraordinary.

Lending a Helping

Hand to other

People in need

Is just something,

In my heart, that

I know needs

To be done.

It's important to offer a
Helping hand to the next
Generation of young
people coming up behind
you, all the while, doing it
with a desire of sympathy,
To help the fallen
When it is not in their
power to help themselves.

My mom and dad
Taught me from a
Very early age to
always lend a helping
hand to anyone in
need.

Europe and
The United States
Are better off
Extending a helping
Hand to those who
Know best rather
Than dictating to
Them an unfamiliar
Future.

Helping Hands

Can Make New Friends.

Reach Out!

For the World

is in Need

And Not Everyone

Can.

Lending a Hand

To Those in Need

Can be accomplished

By even the Smallest

Of Deeds.

Lending a Hand

Can be done

In Countless ways.

With an Open Heart

Anything is Possible.

At Some Point
In our lives
Everybody needs
A Helping Hand.
Take a Look at
At Your Fellow Man.

When You Lend

A Hand

You make a

Friend and

Share a part of

Your Heart

With

Helping Hands

We make

New Friends.

Helping a person

Succeed in their journey

And reach their goals

Brings you both

To a better place.

I am sad to say
That our time
Together
Has come
To an end
But, now let's
Go out and Lend
A Helping Hand.

Sincerely,

Charles Preston Fletcher